SHAQUILLE O'NEAL

★

LARRY JOHNSON

Also by Richard J. Brenner

BASKETBALL SUPERSTARS ALBUM 1993
BASEBALL SUPERSTARS ALBUM 1993
FOOTBALL SUPERSTARS ALBUM 1993
THE WORLD SERIES THE GREAT CONTESTS
THE COMPLETE SUPER BOWL STORY Games I–XXVII
MICHAEL JORDAN
WAYNE GRETZKY

Please see the back pages of this book for details on how to order these and other titles

SHAQUILLE O'NEAL

★

LARRY JOHNSON

RICHARD J. BRENNER

EAST END PUBLISHING, LTD.
SYOSSET, NY

To Jason, Halle, and Anita, with love and thanks. And with love, too, to my mother, Betty Brenner, and my sister, Linda Brenner. Thank you all for your help and encouragement.

And to all the girls and boys of the world, may you always play in happiness.

SHAQUILLE O'NEAL * LARRY JOHNSON

ISBN: 0-943404-20-0

First Printing / August 1993

Photo credits: All of the front and back cover photos were taken by Brian Drake and supplied by SPORT-SCHROME EAST/WEST.
Cover design by Stephen Bell.

This book is published by East End Publishing, Ltd., 54 Alexander Dr., Syosset, NY 11791.

Mr. Brenner is also available to speak to student groups. For details contact East End Publishing, Ltd., 54 Alexander Drive, Syosset, NY 11791, (516) 364-6383.

Contents

SHAQUILLE O'NEAL

1

Little Warrior

On March 6, 1972, Lucille O'Neal gave birth to a boy and named him Shaquille Rashaun, which means "Little Warrior" in Arabic. "I wanted my children to have unique names," said Lucille, who also gave beautiful names to Shaquille's younger sisters, La Teefah and Ayesha, and his little brother, Jamel. "To me, just by having a name that means something makes you special." Because Shaquille's mother and father, Philip Harrison, didn't get married until after he was born, Lucille decided to give her baby her maiden name. Later on, the couple decided not to change Shaquille's name to Harrison, because Lucille wanted someone to carry on O'Neal's family name.

While Shaquille's mom loved his name, it made him the target for a lot of teasing while he was growing up. Like Kermit the Frog finding out that being green isn't easy, Shaquille discovered that there is sometimes a price to pay for being different. "I always got teased. Teased a lot about my name, teased about my size. I'd beat them up, and then it was hard to make friends because people thought I was mean."

One day, though, Shaquille, with a little helpful advice from his mom, realized people would continue to pull his chain until he slipped the leash off by refusing to bite at their tauntings. "One day I just woke up and stopped after my mom told me, 'A man would just say, 'yeah,' and walk away.'"

Eventually, Shaquille got to like his name just fine. "It fits. You know, Michael Jordan, Patrick Ewing, Dominique Wilkins, Larry Bird, Shaquille O'Neal. I think I have a born basketball name."

One day, while Shaquille was in his first year of college, he heard that a couple in nearby Geismer, Louisiana had named their baby Shaquille O'Neal Long, and he became so excited that he drove straight over to Long's home and had his picture taken with the baby. "I love kids because they're cute," explained Shaquille. "They're cute and helpless, so you have to take care of them. For me, I still do stuff that I did as a kid because, hey, I'm still a kid."

2

White as a Ghost

Shaquille spent his earliest years in the city of Newark, New Jersey, living in a project within an urban ghetto, just across the Hudson River from New York City. But whenever his father, an army sergeant, was transferred the entire family moved with him.

All of that moving around taught Shaquille how to make friends with different types of people, and gave him the confidence to handle himself in all sorts of situations. But the downside to all that moving was that Shaquille never had enough time to get too close to anyone. "I didn't ever really have a best friend."

When Shaquille was 10 the family moved from Newark to an army base in Germany. "The best part for me was just getting out of the city," said Shaquille. "Where I come from, there are lots of bad things going down, like drugs and gangs. When I was a kid, I was kind of a juvenile delinquent, but my father always stayed on top of me. Being a drill sergeant, he had to discipline his troops. Then he'd come home and discipline me."

"I always told Shaquille the world has too many clowns and followers. What he needed to be was a leader. He'd see guys hanging out on the corner, and he'd know they were followers. I told him I'd whup him rather than have the guys on the corner whup him. I told him there's no half-steppin' in this life."

Shaquille's dad didn't necessarily wait to come home to make sure that his son was toeing the line. "I used to always tell Shaquille, 'Don't be surprised where you see me next.' I used to drop in at shcool when we were stationed in Germany and watch his classes, just to see what he was up to. One time I went by the school and he was in the classroom banging chairs together. He looked up and saw me and turned white as a ghost," laughed the sergeant.

"I finally got tired and tried it his way," said Shaquille. "It worked. Thank goodness I had parents who loved me enough to stay on my case."

3

"You Can't Dunk, Man"

Shaquille's dad was also his first coach, teaching him the fundamentals of both basketball and football at the base in Germany. Shaquille, who was bigger than all of the other kids his age, might have stuck with football, but one day a hard tackle to his knee convinced him to abandon ship. "That tackle told me I should give up football."

Shaquille grew so fast that he had shot all the way up to 6-6 by the time he was 13. "We'd buy him pants on the post on Saturday, and the next Friday they wouldn't fit," recalls his dad.

Being so tall embarrassed Shaquille so much, he used to slouch to make himself look smaller. "My parents told me to be proud, but I wasn't," said Shaquille. "I didn't know I was special for a long time. I just wanted to be normal."

The rapid growth also didn't do anything for Shaquille's coordination. "I was awkward, falling down all the time." And what was most disheartening to Shaquille was that despite his size he couldn't even dunk a basketball.

One day Shaquille heard that Dale Brown, the basketball coach at Louisiana State University, was at the base conducting a basketball clinic. So Shaquille went up to Brown and asked the coach if he could suggest any exercises that would help him to jump higher.

Brown looked up at Shaquille and assumed that he was in the army. "What rank are you, soldier?" When Shaquille answered that he was only 13, Brown started thinking ahead to how tall Shaquille might be by the time he was ready to start college, and decided to go talk to his dad. As it happened, Shaquille's dad was sitting in a sauna, but Brown, hot on the trail of a very tall prospect, just walked right into the heated room, without even stopping to take off his clothes.

Although Shaquille was still four years away from attending any college, and Brown didn't know if he was really a player, the coach was so intriqued by Shaquille's size that he wanted to plant a seed in Sergeant Harrison's mind—just in case.

But before Brown could get too far into the sales pitch, Shaquille's dad cut him off. The 6–5 sergeant didn't have anything against basketball; in fact, he even played hoops himself at Essex Community College in Jersey City. But he wanted Brown to understand that he was more interested in the development of Shaquille's mind than his basketball skills. "I'm concerned with my son's intellect and education first, and basketball only second. If you're still interested, then maybe we'll talk some day."

Shortly after Brown's visit to the base, Shaquille was outside shooting around by himself when all of a sudden it finally happened. "I just went up and dunked. It was a weak dunk, but I was like, 'Man. I just dunked.' I went to tell everybody, but they didn't believe me because they knew I had bad knees and thought I couldn't jump over a pencil."

And after Shaquille finally persuaded the other kids to follow him back to the bucket for a demonstration of his newfound dunking ability, he shot blanks. "I couldn't do it again. Everybody just walked away saying, 'You can't dunk, man.' "

4

Undefeated

Although Shaquille started to make rapid progress on the court over the next couple of years, he wasn't daydreaming about a slam-dunking career in the NBA. Shaquille had become a big fan of "Fame," a television series set in New York City that followed the fictional lives of a group of teenagers and their teachers at a performing arts high school. In those days, Shaquille spent a lot more time on his break dancing than he did on his fast break, as he put in countless hours spinning on his head while dreaming of becoming a dancer.

By 1987, when Shaquille was 15 years old, his dad was transferred state-side to Fort Sam Houston, so Shaquille finished his last two years of high school at Cole High in San Antonio, Texas. While Shaquille had put up big numbers playing at the base school in Germany, Dave Maduram, the basketball coach at Cole, wasn't impressed. "A lot of kids come in from Germany, and they have these big stats that don't mean anything. Shaquille, though, he could do everything he said he could do."

What Shaquille proceeded to do, for openers, was lead Cole to a 32-1 record in his junior year. Then Shaquille took a giant step forward the following summer in a high school all-star game against Matt Wenstrom, a 7-footer from Houston. "I just kept dunking and dunking," recalled Shaquille, who may have been fueled by some leftover anger that he was carrying around from an argument he had had with his dad the day before the game. "The next day people were calling me the best prep school center in the nation."

When Shaquille returned to Cole for his senior season, he was filled with confidence in his own abilities. And then he went out and justified those feelings by averaging 39 points per game while leading Cole to a 36-0 record and the AAA Texas State title. Shaquille, who was named to the *Parade* magazine All-American team, even received the stamp of approval from John Wooden, the former UCLA coach, who had coached Hall-of-Fame centers Kareem Abdul-Jabbar and Bill Walton, and is considered by many people to be the greatest college coach of all time. "There was no question in my mind that he was going to be a star in college, and go on to the pros and have an outstanding career," said Wooden, who had coached the Bruins to seven straight NCAA championships from 1967-1973. "From a physical standpoint, he had all the things you could want. And when I got to meet him, I thought that he was an outstanding young man in all respects, not just as a basketball player."

As one of the most sought-after recruits in the country, Shaquille had a large choice of colleges from which to choose. After careful consideration, he decided to accept a scholarship offer from Dale Brown, the coach from LSU whom Shaquille had met in Germany before he had been able to dunk. "Other coaches were telling me, 'You'll be in *Sports Illustrated*, you'll start right away.' But Coach Brown never told me anything like that," said Shaquille, who appreciated Brown's soft-sell approach.

Although Shaquille discussed the choices with his parents, the final call belonged to him. Lucille and Philip had provided the love and discipline that Shaquille had needed to grow straight and become his own person, free of the tyranny of the streets, and strong enough to make important decisions independently. As Shaq's dad put it, "That was him alone. We pushed the boat away the day he decided to go there. We told him, 'Go out there and take what we taught you and what you learned in life, and apply it and do what you have to do.' "

5

Unfulfilled Expectations

From the moment that Shaquille agreed to go to LSU, a lot of people, including Coach Brown, began talking about bringing a national championship to Baton Rouge. "I made a mistake by adding to all the preseason hype," said Brown. "We weren't mentally prepared to handle the delusions of grandeur."

That 1989–90 Tiger team was loaded with talent, starting with super-soph Chris Jackson, the sharp-shooting guard who had set an all-time NCAA freshman scoring record by averaging 30.2 points per game the previous year. And Shaquille was joining a front line that already boasted another 7-footer, Stanley Roberts, who was a year older than Shaquille and a fine offensive player.

They were so good, in fact, that one by one they would all become high first-round picks in future NBA drafts. But as a team, they didn't come close to living up to the preseason raves. "When I signed here, I saw Chris and Stanley and myself and some other talented players and I thought to myself, 'We're going all the way,'" recalled Shaquille. "We were supposed to win every game, but every game turned into a challenge."

The Tigers didn't even win the Southeast Conference title, finishing in a second-place tie with a 12–6 conference record, before they ended their season with a 94–91 loss to a Dennis-Scott-and-Kenny-Anderson-led Georgia Tech team in the second round of the NCAA tournament.

Part of the problem for the Tigers' disappointing 23–9 season might have been unrealistic expectations. Then there was the fact that Brown had had to undergo on-the-job training when it came to coaching people as large as Shaquille and Roberts. "I had to find things out about coaching big men. That was a new experience for me," acknowledged Brown, who never did figure out an effective way to use his Twin Towers.

Another part of the problem was that too many people had read their preseason press clippings and didn't work as hard as they should have, including the coach. "I did the worst job of my entire 34 years of coaching," said Brown afterwards. "They were so talented that I thought I could just sit back and watch them play," admitted the coach. "The reason we had an up-and-down season is that we didn't play together as a team," added Shaquille.

As an individual, Shaquille also had his ups and downs. Defensively, he had an instant impact, setting a single-season SEC record with 115 blocked shots, averaging 3.6 per game, sixth best in the country. Shaquille also swept the boards clean 12 times a game on average to rank ninth in the nation in rebounding. Scoring-wise, Shaquille was less of a factor, as the offense was designed to go to Jackson as the first option and then Roberts. Shaquille had to do most of his scoring on rim-rattling dunks off of offensive rebounds.

Among the highlights of Shaquille's first year of college ball was a 17-point, 14-rebound effort that helped the Tigers topple Larry Johnson and UNLV, the team that went on to capture the 1990 NCAA championship. His best effort, though, came in a 148-141 overtime win over Loyola of Marymount in which Shaquille posted an awesome triple-double—recording double-digit numbers in three different categories—as he skied for 20 points, pulled down 24 rebounds, and blocked 12 shots, breaking the single-game SEC record of 10 that he had set earlier in the season. "That's the perfect style," said a smiling Shaquille. "Loyola and UNLV, they make the game fun. I don't like being in a slow game, standing still."

6

Mr. Robinson's Neighborhood

Another high point of Shaquille's freshman year occurred during spring break when he attended a San Antonio Spurs practice and met their All-Star center, David Robinson. A few days before they met, Shaquille had become intrigued with Robinson's style of play after watching the Spurs play a New York Knicks team that featured another 7-footer, Patrick Ewing. "Ewing used to be my idol, but after I saw big Dave dunk on him, I started liking Robinson. Robinson is a new breed. Most 7-footers are slow and can't dribble very well, but Robinson is fast and he can handle the ball. There's only two players like that on this earth—David Robinson and Shaquille O'Neal."

It turned out that Robinson was also a big fan of Shaquille's. "I saw him play all year on television. The thing that I really noticed about him was the aggressiveness that he had on the court. He takes the ball strong to the hole all the time, and he is a tremendous rebounder. Those are the things you look for in a player when he gets to college. I know that it took me about two or three years to learn those things. He showed all those things as a *freshman*," said Robinson, who had been the NCAA Player of the Year in his senior season at the Naval Academy in 1987.

"I'm really impressed with the impact he's made in such a short period. He has a tremendous future. I've got to get ready for him in a few years."

Before Shaquille left the practice session, however, Robinson delivered a king-sized needle to Shaquille. "What happened in the NCAA tourney? You had a great team." And then Robinson advised Shaquille to stay in school and not be tempted to enter the NBA too early.

The talk about Shaquille leaving LSU for the NBA had begun almost as soon as he had entered the school. And while there were still a lot of rough edges to his game, it was obvious even then that Shaquille was a superstar in the making and could earn a multimillion-dollar salary in the NBA. "The thing that's so shocking is that there's still so much room for improvement," said Kentucky coach Rick Pitino. "He's the only player I've seen in quite some time that would be the number one pick in the NBA draft in any of his four years that he decided to enter it. After a year or so of NBA competition, you'd be looking at Hakeem Olajuwan [the All-Star center of the Houston Rockets]."

Although Shaquille had no intention of leaving school at that point, he still would daydream from time to time about the fame and the money that lay ahead. "I'm only human," acknowledged Shaquille. "I have dreams like anyone else. I'd like to have a Wheaties commercial. I'd like to have an 'Air Shaq' commercial, I'd like to give kids a positive message.

"I'd buy my mother a big house and a Mercedes. I'd buy my father a Jaguar. I'd buy my family a big van with a VCR, Nintendo for the kids, phone, answering machine, stuff like that. I'd buy myself a Mercedes, a nice house, and throw the rest in the bank."

That was the dream, but the reality was that neither Shaquille nor his parents had any intention of putting dollars before a college education. They all had a strong belief that there is more to life than the goodies that dollars can buy, and that there are some things—like a well-developed, educated mind—that money just can't buy. "We've had hard times our whole lives," said Shaquille's dad. "We can wait a few more years." And besides, Shaquille realized that when he left college for the NBA, he'd be going to work. "The way I see it, the NBA is all business. It's a job." And Shaquille wasn't ready to give up the good life of a student-athlete. "I want to stay in school and get my degree."

7

"Oh, Nellie!"

Shaquille gave an indication that he was about to emerge as a bona fide superstar during the summer, when he led a team of southern all-stars to the gold medal in the Olympic Festival in Minneapolis. Shaquille completely rewrote the Festival record book, as he notched the first triple-double in the history of the tournament, while averaging 24.5 points and 13.8 rebounds per game.

After Shaquille's string of eye-opening performances, which earned him the Most Valuable Player award, he acted as though people had a right to expect the spectacular. "During the competition, I think I've been as dominant as I should be. I mean, I'm 7-foot-1 and 285 pounds. Seven foot means dominance. I've always been taught that it's my court. I use it, I control it. It's my place."

Shaquille spent the rest of the summer back home in San Antonio, playing pickup games for a few hours every day, and did calf raises way into the night to increase the explosiveness of his lift-off.

By the time he returned to Baton Rouge for the start of his sophomore year, Shaquille knew that the Tigers had lost a lot of talent and that the team would go only as far as he could carry it. Gone was Chris Jackson, who had entered the NBA draft the previous spring and been snapped up by the Denver Nuggets, the third player chosen. Also gone was Stanley Roberts, who decided to play for pay in Europe because he couldn't maintain passing grades.

Although two-thirds of the Tigers' Golden Triangle had pulled up stakes, Shaquille was still ready to prospect for an NCAA championship. "Those guys are gone, but I still dream about going to the Final Four. We've lost a lot of talent, but talent isn't everything—just look at last year. I know it's going to be more difficult this year, but it's my job to make sure we play hard, we play together, and we play to win."

Just in case Shaquille didn't have enough pressure on his young shoulders, before the season even began nearly a dozen magazines featured him on the cover and announced that he was the sport's next superstar. Then Dale Brown turned the heat up even higher on Shaquille's thermostat by appointing him a co-captain and telling him, "Your role is going to have to change if we're going to have a chance. I hate to put pressure on you—I know you're only 18 years old —but we're going to you. If we're going back to the NCAA tournament, you have to be the man."

That was a heavy load to pile on a teenager, but Shaquille never flinched or complained. "If people want to focus on me, that's fine, I can take it. I'm not going to let that sort of pressure get to me. I can't read about how great I am, I have to go out and prove it."

Although Brown had anointed Shaquille as the leader and focal point of the team, the coach knew that his budding young star wasn't, as yet, a fully developed player. "He's got to learn how to play prevent defense. Keep people from getting the ball. He's also got to cut down his fouls," said Brown, noting that Shaquille had fouled out of nine games as a freshman. "He has to understand that he needs more offensive moves, like a hook shot, for example." Since Brown himself had such limited experience in coaching big players, he decided to bring in Bill Walton to tutor Shaquille for the upcoming season.

Walton, one of the best centers to ever lace a pair of sneakers, had led UCLA to two consecutive NCAA championships in 1972 and 1973, and the Portland Trail Blazers to the 1977 NBA title. Walton has always been regarded as a brainy basketball player and team leader who, before injuries hobbled him, had been a 20-per-game point producer, as well as an excellent rebounder and shot blocker, and just possibly the best all-time passer out of the pivot.

Shaquille was thrilled when he heard that Walton was coming to work with him. "When Coach Brown told me Bill Walton was coming here, I thought, 'Damn, Big Red is coming to work with me.'"

After five days of practice, the red-headed Walton knew that Shaquille was the Real Deal. "I'm immensely impressed. He's an outstanding young man who has an unlimited future ahead of him, and that's a great thing, because he's such a hard worker and has such a great attitude."

Walton didn't want to get caught up in comparing Shaquille to established NBA centers. "Don't fall into a habit of calling him the next Hakeem Olajuwan," he advised. "This is the first Shaquille O'Neal." But Walton did compare Shaquille's jumping ability, the very thing he had worked on during the summer, to that of All-NBA forward Charles Barkley. "Shaquille has that quick, unrestrainable explosion, like Barkley. This guy may have the physical talent and personal discipline to become the best. But like I told Shaquille, it's not the numbers or the stats, it's how he controls the flow of the game."

Shaquille justified all of Walton's high expectations by turning in a spectacular season in which he piled up the stats *and* dictated the course of games, while leaving no doubt as to who was the reigning big man in college basketball.

Shaquille caught the attention of basketball fans everywhere when the Tigers collided with Arizona in a nationally televised game early in the 1990-91 season. The Wildcats, who came to Baton Rouge as the No. 2 ranked team in the country, featured a skyscraper front line that included Sean Rooks, Chris Mills, and Brian Williams and was considered to be the biggest and best front court this side of the NBA.

But Shaquille, with 29 points, 14 rebounds, and six key blocks, demolished the Tucson Skyline, while leading the No. 18 ranked Tigers to a 92–82 upset win that sent television announcer Dick Vitale into squeals of delight.

"That's unstoppable!" shrieked Vitale after one rim-rattling dunk. "Just throw it up. Just throw the rock up in the air, flip it up and I'll finish it off." After Shaquille had banked in a short jump shot, Vitale really revved his engine. "That's an *amazing* move. That's Hakeem Olajuwan, David Robinson, Patrick Ewing."

Shaquille and Vitale were just getting warmed up, though, when Shaquille grabbed an offensive rebound and rammed the ball through the nets with a windmill motion that seemed to lift Vitale out of his seat. "I mean this is *frightening*. This is awesome baby. *Awesome*."

Shaquille closed out the game by finishing off a coast-to-coast trip with a resounding dunk and celebration dance that he later told reporters was called the Shaq-de-Shaq, making sure that they knew to spell it with a "q" rather than a "ck." And Vitale seemed to break out into an accompaniment of Shaq's dance as he sang out, "It's over. It's over. Look at Shaquille do the dance. It's awesome. Look at this. Take a look. Seven-one. Oooo-Nellie!"

While Vitale couldn't get over what he had just seen, Arizona coach Lute Olson had seen more than enough. "There's no question he's the best big man in the country, and it's not even a close call."

"The tapes don't do him justice," added Arizona forward Chris Mills. "It's kind of amazing to see him in person."

Going up against Arizona had charged Shaq's competitive battery. "I'd heard stuff from out there that I was just another player, that I was too young. I wanted to show I could play with anybody." The game that Shaq wanted most of all, though, wasn't on LSU's schedule. "Georgetown. Alonzo

Mourning was the guy I had always heard about. I've always wanted to measure myself against the best."

Because the Hoyas weren't on the Tigers' schedule, Shaq didn't get to face off against Mourning until they entered the NBA as the league's two top rookies a couple of years down the road. In the meantime, though, Shaquille got all the incentive he needed from Jamal Mashburn, the hot-shot freshman forward from SEC-rival Kentucky. Mashburn got Shaquille growling like Tony the Tiger when he volunteered his opinion that Shaq wasn't any better than "all right" and that he could definitely be "stopped." Shaquille responded to those challenging words with an in-your-face performance that included 28 points, 17 rebounds, and four blocked shots, which caused Mashburn to totally reconsider his assessment of Shaq's attacking powers. "O'Neal belongs in a higher league," said the humbled freshman. Kentucky coach Rick Pitino agreed that Shaquille was, indeed, physically ready to play at another level. "The NBA team that gets him will get an all-star, an immediate-impact franchise player. He could take an expansion team and make it a playoff team right away."

Shaquille put an exclamation mark on his statement to Mashburn in a rematch against Kentucky, the first-place team in the SEC. The Shaq-man hit his first nine shots on the way to a 33-point, 16-rebound, seven-stuffs game that propelled the Tigers to a 107-88 whipping of the Wildcats. "We couldn't handle Shaquille O'Neal," said Pitino. "He's a dominating player at both ends of the court. He's simply the best college player in America."

8

To Be Like Mike

The difference in Shaq's play between his frosh and sopho-more seasons was staggering. As Dale Brown noted, "He's the most improved, outstanding athlete I've ever coached. There's something new in his game all the time."

As a freshman, Shaquille had relied on his immense physi-cal attributes to overpower people on the offensive boards, while becoming a menacing presence at the defensive end. But in his second season of college ball, Shaq had become a total force. "There's no comparison to when he was a fresh-man," observed Vanderbilt coach Eddie Folgher after Sha-quille had scored 34 points and pulled down 11 boards while leading LSU to ao 87-70 vanquishing of Vandy. "He's vastly improved offensively. Last year, if he didn't dunk, you felt you had a decent chance of having him miss. Now, he's at a point where an eight-foot turnaround is almost automatic. It's kind of scary."

"Trying to stop Shaq now is a joke," observed Georgia coach Hugh Durham after Shaquille had exploded for 34 points, ripped off 16 rebounds, and blocked seven shots while leading LSU past the Bulldogs, 83–76. "Last year you could play behind him and know he wasn't going to get the ball from those other guys. Now Shaq may be unguardable."

Although Shaquille's scoring touch had caught a lot of people by surprise, he wasn't one of them. "I always knew how to shoot. I averaged 39 points a game in my last season in high school. But last year we had Chris and Stanley and that wasn't my role. Everybody said my shot was flat, but most of my shots were fadeaways in the paint off offensive rebounds, with a hand in my face. Otherwise, I didn't get many shots."

It wasn't only that Shaq's scoring was way up or that his other stats were also headed skyward, it was that he was like a mighty dam, controlling the flow of games and dictating the style and tempo at which they were played. "He makes you play so differently," explained Tennessee coach Wade Houston. "It's hard to play the way you normally do because he's so capable of dominating the game. You can throw the game plan out the window."

Shaquille's fame and acclaim continued to swell as he became the most closely followed college athlete on the planet. In January, he was featured on the cover of *Sports Illustrated* and called, "The best sophomore center I've ever seen," by NBA super-scout Marty Blake.

But neither the praise nor the publicity turned Shaq's head or caused him to buy bigger hats. And he never said or did anything that would demean or embarass any of his less-talented teammates. "I think I'm a team player. I like to block shots. I like to get the ball and make the long outlet pass. I just like to win."

"He doesn't have an ego to feed," noted Coach Brown. "He breathes life into a team. Some superstars suck the breath out of a team. They don't make anybody better. Shaquille makes everybody better."

Somehow, at only 18 years of age, Shaquille had found a way to celebrate himself without diminishing others, while maintaining a perspective and even a sense of humor about what was happening in his life. Shaquille didn't shrink from wearing a baseball cap that a friend had stenciled with the inscription, "I AM THE SHAQNIFICENT." And his front license plate had his jersey number, 32, on it, while the back plate read, "Shaquille the Deal." "I realize I'm different. I also realize that I can handle myself well, and I don't let the publicity get to my head."

Shaquille also respected the fact that other people had feelings and jobs to do, including the hordes of hungry media who were constantly feeding the public's sense of awe about him. "See, I can take it all one of two ways. I can be nice and talk to the media, or I can walk around arrogant and be Billy Badbutt. But what fun would that be?

"People don't like a smart butt. Only a few people like Bill Laimbeer, but everybody likes Michael Jordan. I want to be like Mike."

9
Player of the Year

The overwhelming importance of Shaq's presence in the LSU lineup was never more obvious then when a hairline fracture of his right leg forced him to miss a regular-season-ending loss to Mississippi State and a first-round SEC tournament loss to Auburn, a team that the Tigers trounced by 37 points only two weeks and one player earlier.

The announcement that Shaquille would be back in time to play against the University of Connecticut in the opening round of the NCAA tournament did not necessarily send shivers of delight down the spine of U Conn coach Jim Calhoun. "I don't remember us facing a guy who averages 27.7 points, almost 15 rebounds, and also blocks shots. He can change the complexion of a game completely."

Although Shaquille lived up to his advanced billing by bagging 27 points, 16 boards, and five blocked shots, he didn't get enough help from his teammates and the Tigers went down to defeat, 79–62, finishing their season at 20–9.

"Back in my younger days, I used to cry," said Shaquille. "But now there's nothing to do but go home and do homework, get good grades, and live my life. There's nothing else I can do."

Shaquille had done all that he could in leading the Tigers to a share of the Southeast Conference regular season title, and the fact that he couldn't carry them all the way to a Final Four appearance was no fault of his. Shaquille had slammed and jammed for 27.6 points per game, nearly double his freshman average, led the nation in rebounding with a 14.7 average, and finished third in blocked shots with a national-sophomore-record 5.0 per game. He had been LSU's leading scorer 21 times, and its leading rebounder 24 times, in the 27 games in which he had played, while breaking his own conference record with 140 blocked shots and becoming the first player to lead the SEC in scoring, rebounding, field goal percentage, and blocked shots in the same season. "Shaquille is dominant in the game because he's an athlete," said Georgia coach Hugh Durham. "He's not just big. There are a lot of guys out there that are 7 feet and 285 pounds, but they are not dominant players. Some of them are good, some aren't, some don't even go out for basketball."

"O'Neal is a men among boys at this level," summed up Auburn's Tommy Joe Eagles, who, like the other coaches in the SEC, found going up against his Shaqnificance about as much fun as a trip to the dentist.

The sportswriters and sportscasters around the country added their stamp of approval to Shaquille's sensational sophomore season by selecting him as the Associated Press College Basketball Player of the Year. Shaq, who beat out UNLV's senior teammates Larry Johnson and Stacey Augmon, became only the fourth sophomore to win the prestigious Adolph F. Rupp Trophy, joining Bill Walton, who won the award three straight years starting in 1972; Virginia's Ralph Sampson in 1981; and De Paul's Mark Aguirre in 1980. Kareem Abdul-Jabbar, when he was still called Lew Alcindor, also won the award as a sophomore, in 1967, but that was before it was named for Rupp, the late-great coach of the Kentucky Wildcats.

"I'm not too thrilled about awards," said Shaq, who was also named Player of the Year by United Press International, LA Gear, and *Sports Illustrated.* "But I am glad that I have my name next to the elite players, such as Patrick Ewing, Bill Walton and Kareem."

Shaquille also took the opportunity to put to rest the increasing speculation that he was about to end his college career. "I'm looking forward to coming back and playing in college again next year. There's a lot of things I need to learn. I'm not ready to turn pro yet. I watched Patrick Ewing kill the Spurs on TV. I'm not ready for Patrick. I need to work on my hook shot."

The speculation that Shaquille might leave school early had increased as teams started to double- and triple-team him, stifling his offensive development and taking some of the fun out of the game. Georgetown coach John Thompson, a former college and NBA center, agreed that the rules of college basketball were too restrictive when it came to big centermen. "The NBA's far more conducive for big men, and if we don't do something about it, we'll discourage post players from staying in college."

The thought of playing in the NBA, where zone defenses are illegal, was very appealing to Shaquille. "That would be kind of nice, having just one man on me. But that's not how they play the game in college, so there's no sense in thinking about it. I'm not a complainer."

Shaquille and his family had also become alarmed at the hard, deliberate fouls that had been committed against him as some teams resorted to dirty tactics to combat Shaq's superior abilities. To his credit, Shaq retaliated with talent rather than thuggery. "When a guy is out there pushing and shoving on me, it isn't hard to keep my temper. What I want to do is slam on him. That's the best way to handle it."

Shaq, a very competitive individual, also had to weigh whether or not he could reach his goal of playing in the Final Four with the diminished level of talent on the Tigers team. Maybe it would be more challenging to step into the NBA arena and go head-to-head against Robinson, Ewing, and Olajuwan. And it would certainly be nice to shower his family with the presents that NBA dollars would buy.

After weighing all the factors, however, Shaquille made his decision to return to LSU, and, in the process, pleased his parents greatly. "I'm really glad he's going back," said Shaquille's dad. "I don't think you can ever get enough education." And Philip wasn't in any great hurry to cash in on his son's talent. "We haven't had any money in 18 years, and we're not in any rush for it now. You've got to keep your priorities in order and stay focused. Education, that's the main thing."

10

When the Fun Stops

By the end of Shaq's sophomore season, he had become the top pro prospect in college ball. "I can't take my eyes off him," swooned Don Nelson, the coach and general manager of the Golden State Warriors. "I think I'm in love."

But instead of polishing his trophies, or reading his press clippings, Shaquille began developing the abilities that he hoped would take him to the next level. "I don't think I have that much talent," explained Shaq. "I couldn't always shoot. I couldn't always dunk. I had to practice. I don't believe in talent. I believe in working hard."

It was that attitude, as much as Shaq's size and ability, and the promise of even more to come, that had the pro scouts drooling. "He seems to understand that you need to work to improve," said Brad Greenberg, the director of player personnel for the Portland Trail Blazers. "He's as exciting a big-man prospect as I can recall. And he's just starting to tap his potential."

Shaq spent the summer before his junior year working on different aspects of his game so that he wouldn't be limited to playing in the paint, where he almost always drew double- and triple-teams. Shaq wanted to style his game along the lines of Duke's 6–11 center, Christian Laettner, who played more like a forward, using his mobility to drive to the hoop and pop 3-pointers, as well as play in the box. Shaq had been completely outplayed by Laettner in a game won by Duke the previous year, and then had watched Laettner lead the Blue Devils to Shaq's dream, the NCAA championship. Laettner's versatility is what would also earn him a spot over Shaquille the following summer on the Dream Team, the 1992 gold-medal-winning Olympic basketball squad.

"I like to run," noted Shaquille. "I don't like that slow, turtle-like game. Most 7-tooters can't dribble, or run and jump. Usually they just post up. I've worked on my all-around game. I was kind of hoping that Coach Brown would put in a new offense so I could have kind of a Christian Laettner freedom to drive and penetrate, step outside and shoot the trey—work on my jump shot. I can shoot, bro, my 'J' is on."

Shaq didn't get his wish to play a diversified game, however, because Brown was too occupied with trying to piece together a competitive team, and felt that Shaq's game was better suited to a traditional low-post offense. "We want him to develop another shot," said Brown. "But we don't want to take away his power game by having him play a Kareem Abdul-Jabbar skyhook game."

In addition to shouldering his disappointment about Brown's decision, Shaq also had to deal with the exaggerated expectations that his sophomore season had inspired. "Shaquille's in a tough position," said teammate Vernel Singleton. "If he doesn't get like 28 points and 15 rebounds, then people might say he had a bad game. That's a tough position to be in."

The hardest part of playing with mostly mediocre players was that there wasn't anybody to relieve the pressure on Shaquille. Brown hadn't found any reliable 3-point scorers who could draw defenders outside and prevent defenses from collapsing around Shaquille. "About midway through my sophomore season, everyone found out about me, and they started to use three or four guys on me. It hasn't been the same since," said Shaquille, who was having the fun sapped out of the sport he loved playing. "I try to keep my head up high and play on, but sometimes when I see the room that Patrick Ewing gets, I wonder what it would be like."

Shaq, though, weathered all the storms and turned in a second successive All-American season, in which he led the nation in blocked shots, finished second in rebounding, and averaged 24.1 points per game. He also managed to almost single-handedly lead the Tigers into the second round of the NCAA tournament, where they were bounced out by Indiana despite a heroic 36-point, 12-rebound, 5-blocked-shot effort by his Shaqnificance.

Shaq even drew the ultimate in praise from Hall of Famer Wilt Chamberlain, who had once scored *100* points in a single NBA game and who is, arguably, the best center to ever play the game. "He's the closest thing to me that I've ever seen in college ball. He's like a Wilt Chamberlain reincarnated." Shaq's play also impressed Dick Harp, who had coached the Big Dipper at the University of Kansas. "It's only a matter of time until Shaquille's a great player. My wife could sit down, take a look at him, and tell you that."

But after the season was finished, Shaquille decided to bring his college career to a close and enter the NBA draft. "I played my heart out for LSU, but I was getting nowhere. It wasn't fun playing anymore. I didn't leave because of money. I left because it had stopped being fun. I was taught at a young age that if you're not having fun at what you're doing, then it's time to do something else."

11

Rookie of the Year

For the first time since 1985, when Patrick Ewing was the No. 1 player on every team's wish list, there was no doubt who the first pick of the draft was going to be. Despite the fact that there was a bumper crop of college talent from which to choose, including Alonzo Mourning and Christian Laettner, as soon as Shaquille announced that he was coming out, the draft became the Shaquille O'Neal sweepstakes. "He's one of the top five centers in the NBA right now, and he may move up by the end of the week," joked Jerry Reynolds, the director of player personnel for the Sacramento Kings. "There hasn't been anybody coming into the league who has made this kind of stir in a long time, maybe since Kareem. People usually talk about college players having a tough time adjusting to the physical nature of the NBA. In this case, the reverse may be true. People in our league may have trouble adjusting to him. He's going to make any of the weaker teams better quickly."

"He's the only person on the immediate horizon who's in the complete-player category of a Larry Bird, Magic Johnson and Michael Jordan," added Fordy Anderson, chief scout for the Boston Celtics.

Although Shaquille had expressed a desire to play in Los Angeles, when he was drafted by the Magic he flew to Orlando, put on some mouse ears, and announced, "I'm going to Disney World and chillin' with Mickey." A month after that visit, Shaq came back and put his signature on a seven-year, 40-million-dollar contract to play basketball for the Orlando Magic.

Despite the fact that he had become the highest paid

player in the history of the sport, and was being compared to its greatest players before he had even played his first NBA game, Shaquille spent most of the summer developing his skills. "I need to work on all of my game, because there is always room for improvement."

Included in Shaq's itinerary was a stop at the famous summer camp for big men in California that is run by 77-year-old Pete Newell, the guru of the game when it comes to working with centers and forwards. Newell, who has seen all of the great big men from George Mikan to Patrick Ewing, was immediately captivated by his newest pupil. "Shaq's got an explosiveness that no one that big has ever had. He has a chance to be a truly unique player."

While Shaquille was on the west coast, he joined in pickup games with NBA players and starred in "A Midsummer Night's Magic," the annual all-star game that Magic Johnson stages to benefit the United Negro College Fund. "He'll be great," declared Magic. "The guy's a monster, a true prime-time player. On one play, Shaq came down on a break, pulled up for a short jumper, missed, but sailed over a big guy, grabbed the ball and slammed the sucker home. We were stunned."

Shaquille scored points with his Orlando teammates before their first practice by agreeing to wear No. 33 instead of trying to coerce forward Terry Catledge into giving up the No. 32 that Shaq had worn at LSU. "He could have come in here and been a jerk, and there wouldn't be anything that any of us could have done about it," said point guard Scott Skiles. "But Shaq's just the opposite and that will help make him better and us better as a team."

And once training camp began, Shaquille quickly convinced everyone that he was the real item. "He's so talented that without learning anything new, he could be an All-Star every year," said veteran Greg Kite, the team's backup center. "But if he picks up all the little things, there might not be a limit. He has a unique set of tools to work with."

Praise like that served to feed the extraordinary expectations regarding Shaquille as an individual, and about how high he could left a team which had ended the previous season with a 21–61 mark, the second worst record in the NBA.

There was so much excitement surrounding Shaq's arrival in the NBA that 180 reporters, from places as far away as France and Japan, had come to cover his first league game. And while Matt Goukas, Orlando's coach during the 1992–93 season, would have liked to shield his prized pupil from all the hype, there was no hiding the fact that Shaquille would be the hub around which the Magic would turn. "We're going inside to Shaq," said Goukas on the eve of Orlando's season opener. And then he added, for emphasis, "We're going to be going to him a lot," secure in the knowledge that he wasn't revealing any state secrets.

But if Shaq was feeling any butterflies about his first regular season NBA game, he wasn't talking about them. "I don't believe in pressure. You go through things step by step, and you don't worry about anything. I know about the expectations, and if I do become a great center like Chamberlain, or Bill Russell [the former Celtic great who led Boston to 11 NBA championships], or Kareem, or Walton, that's good. If not, I'll live a happy life and keep a smile on my face."

Then Shaquille stepped out on the court against the Miami Heat and pulled down 18 rebounds, the most for a rookie in his first game since Bill Walton had taken down 24 boards in his NBA debut in 1974. "There is no doubt that he's a monster," said Miami center Rony Seikaly. "That's like an *understatement.*"

After his first five games Shaquille was leading the league in rebounding (16.4 per game), was tied for fourth in scoring (25.8), was fifth in blocked shots (3.4), and had become the first rookie to ever be named the NBA Player of the Week in his first week in the league. "If this is what's coming out of college these days, I'm out of here," said New Jersey Nets veteran Rick Mahorn.

"In all my years, I've never seen a package of talent like this," added Greg Kite. "Patrick Ewing has a lot of strength, and David Robinson is really quick, but nobody combines the strength and quickness that Shaquille has."

Although Shaq had gotten off to a superstar beginning, he wasn't about to get too full of himself. "The only award I really work for is to help make us a winner. This is a credit to both our coaches and my teammates who helped me get ready for the season."

"I thought I was going to come in and average 10 points and nine rebounds, or something like that," said Shaquille. "But once I got off to a quick start I knew that I could play in this league." And after his first four weeks in the league, Shaquille had also been named the NBA Rookie of the Month and made believers out of everyone who had seen him play. "Before the season, I said I didn't think one guy could just come in here and dominate," said Dave Twardzik, the player personnel director of the Charlotte Hornets. "Well, I was wrong. He's not a perfect player, but the impact he's had is amazing."

"He's going to be unstoppable," said Atlanta Hawks superstar Dominique Wilkins. "He's going to dominate this game. He's doing it now on just raw ability." And that was a really scary thought for the rest of the league, because if Shaq could be so close to being the best in the game when he was still so far away from fulfilling his own outsized potential, then just how great was he going to become after he had gained a year or two of experience?

Shaquille's precious play and radiant personality also made him a favorite with the fans around the league. The fans showed their appreciation by voting him onto the Eastern Conference squad, along with Larry Johnson, Scottie Pippin,

Isiah Thomas, and Michael Jordan. "It will be an honor to play with guys like that," said Shaquille, who out-polled Patrick Ewing by nearly 250,000 votes, and became only the 14th rookie, and the first since Michael Jordan, to earn a starting spot in an NBA All Star game. "I'm happy that the fans like to see me play. I'm 7 feet 1, 300 pounds. I dunk hard. I slide on the floor. I get rebounds. I can dribble the length of the court. And, hey, people like to see that. If I was a fan, I'd want to come and see Shaq play, too."

Shaq had a great time at the All-Star Weekend, and even became the first player to perform a musical act at the NBA's Stay in School Jam on the Saturday before the Game. He sang "What's Up Doc?" with Fu Schnickens, his favorite rap music group. Shaq also made some sweet music during the game, as he jammed for a fast 13 points in 14 first-half minutes. Although Shaq was forced to split playing time equally with Patrick Ewing (maybe because the East coach was Pat Riley, who is also the New York Knicks coach), he didn't complain. "It was just fun being out there, playing with all the great players," said Shaq. "But my best moments were hanging out with Grandmama [Larry Johnson] and Michael [Jordan]. I got my picture taken with them and their autographs."

Shaquille didn't just put up fancy stats or win popularity contents with his awesome stuffs and thunderous dunks, which sometimes brought the backboard down, he also turned the Magic from perennial losers into a competitive team. At the All-Star break the Magic, with a 24–23 record, had already won three more games than they had the previous season. "We're playing real good ball, and there's one reason: the Big Guy. He makes us all better," said Nick Anderson, Orlando's sharp-shooting guard. "The difference is the amount of room we get now, because teams have to double down on Shaq," said small forward Dennis Scott, the Magic's top 3-point shooter.

Part of Shaquille's initiation into the league was going head-to-head against the NBA's other top centers, including Patrick Ewing, with whom he had four epic heavyweight battles that ended in a draw. "He's just so strong. I mean, he is *so* strong," marveled Pat Riley. "You've got to get him out of the paint. Any time he gets the ball with his head under the rim . . . well, you saw what happened." And even though Shaquille dropped two decisions each to David Robinson and Hakeem Olajuwon, he still drew high praise. "He's the new kid on the block, and the sky's the limit," noted Olajuwon.

Shaquille didn't have any problem acknowledging that those three All-Star veterans were more advanced than he was. "They know some things that obviously I don't know because they were born ahead of me. And right now, they can hit the jumper more consistently than I can. That's what makes them so hard to stop. If you slow them down inside, they take you outside and either drive by you, or pull up for the 'J.'

"That's fine. I'll have a jumper one day, too. Right now, I'm just trying to be realistic. When you play 82 games, you're going to have some nights when you dominate, some where you're so-so, and some where you play like you don't belong in the league."

Shaquille also finally got to play against Alonzo Mourning, the player whom he most wanted to measure himself against when the two of them were in college, and the player with whom he is destined to be linked like Magic Johnson and Larry Bird and, from an earlier era, Wilt Chamberlain and Bill Russell. Their first two showdowns turned into classic contests, as each player led his team to one victory while leading his respective team in scoring and rebounding.

Shaquille's duels against the league's other top big men helped give his teammates the confidence to know that, on any given night, the Magic could beat any team in the league, even the two-time defending-NBA-champion Chicago Bulls.

In one of the most memorable games of the season, Shaquille scored 31 points, blocked five shots, and pulled down a season-high 24 rebounds while leading the Magic to a 128–124 overtime victory over the Bulls, despite a 64-point explosion by his Airness. "He's going to be a great player," said Jordan.

"We aren't an automatic playoff team just because of Shaq," said Magic general manager Pat Williams. "But with him we have a chance to compete every night."

The Magic, in fact, just missed the playoffs when they were edged out by the Indiana Pacers, who finished with an identical 41–41 record but won in a tiebreaker. With Shaquille in their lineup, though, the Magic finished the season as the most improved team in the NBA and with a forecast of even brighter days ahead. As Dennis Scott put it, "Now, because of the Big Fellow, we have something to build on."

Shaquille, who was named the NBA Rookie of the Month for November, December, January, and February, was the runaway winner of the Rookie of the Year award, beating Alonzo Mourning by a 96–2 vote by a nationwide panel of sportswriters and broadcasters. "I hope I can get an NBA championship trophy to go along with it," said Shaq, "so that when I retire and have children, I can tell them, 'I was *bad.*'"

Shaq, who finished second in the league in rebounding and blocked shots, fourth in field goal percentage, and eighth in scoring, was the only player in the NBA to rank in the top ten in those four categories. "I was just doing what I was supposed to do," said Shaq, who also became the first rookie to score 1,000 points and record 1,000 rebounds since Buck Williams turned the trick during the 1981–82 season. "At 7–1, 303, you're supposed to go out there and dunk, rebound, and battle. I was just doing my job."

But even as Shaquille was playing down his spectacular rookie accomplishments, he was already pointing to a promise of an even greater future. "I'm going to get better and better at it once I learn this league. I want to get better every year, every month, every game. I'm paid too much money to sit back and get lazy. That's not me. I've got a lot to learn, but one day, I'm going to be *the man* in the league. You can write that down and underline it three times."

12

"Shaq Attaq"

Shaquille has been as big a success off the court as on it. With his awesome athletic potential and pleasing personality, Shaq has been able to sign multi-million dollar deals with companies such as Reebok, Pepsi, Spalding, Kenner Toys, and Classic Cards. Some of the commercials that he's done, such as the "Don't fake the funk on a nasty dunk" Reebok ad in which Shaq doesn't quite measure up to legends Bill Russell, Bill Walton, Wilt Chamberlain or Kareem Abdul Jabbar, have already become classics and increased his ever-growing popularity.

All of the different advertising is linked together by the "Shaq Attaq" symbol, which has the name 'Shaq' superimposed over a silhouette of Shaquille dunking a basketball.

"There's no one in the history of sports that has burst on the scene with such fanfare or anticipation," claims Shaquille's agent, Leonard Armato. "And what's so extraordinary is that he's lived up to the expectations both on and off the court. The potential for Shaquille is unlimited." Or, as Shaq said with a smile, "I'm a very marketable guy. Tall, dark, and handsome. Beautiful smile. Nice. Pretty good player."

Although Shaq has already signed contracts that will pay him at least 70 million dollars, he claims that he won't be adversely affected by his newfound wealth. "Money doesn't make people change. People make people change, and I'm not going to let that happen. The only difference money makes is in material things, like a couple of more cars. I don't like to drink. I never liked the taste of beer. I might drink wine or champagne once a year to celebrate something, but that's it. I'm not going to go out partying and ruin what I've got going. Drugs scare me. If you can't figure out what kind of trouble you've got there, you can't figure out very much at all."

The money has also allowed Shaq to buy a beautiful home in Orlando, and equip it with arcade games and a state-of-the-art music system. "I like toys and I like my music," said the Shaqmeister. And the music that Shaq likes best is rap. In fact, he and teammate and close friend Dennis Scott appeared on the Arsenio Hall television show and performed a rap song with Fu Schnickens. "If basketball doesn't work out, I can always be a rapper," joked Shaq.

But Shaquille also realizes that there's more to life than basketball and good times. "I'm already a rich man, and what I do for a living really isn't work. That's why I don't feel any pressure. Pressure is when you don't know where your next meal is coming from. That's why it makes me mad to see people living on the street."

Shaquille backed up his words by spending his first Thanksgiving in Orlando at a homeless shelter feeding 300 hungry people, some of whom had never even heard of him. "Basketball isn't everything in life. It doesn't make a difference if they know me, as long as they can eat and they're happy.

"Hey, I've eaten on food stamps. When we lived on the 17th floor in the projects in Newark, that's how we bought groceries. These people are just not as fortunate as I am now."

Shaquille also played Santa Claus at Christmas, delivering three truckloads of toys to needy children. And he's also a regular visitor at the Arnold Palmer Hospital for Women and Children. Although the Orlando Magic contracts require players to do some charity work, no one has had to push Shaq into lending a helpful hand. "Nobody has to tell me to go visit a sick baby or help feed the homeless. I want to be big enough to do that for myself. It's something I'll keep on doing.

"Life is always going to be the same for me. I'll always be a down-to-earth person. I'll never forget where I came from, and I'll always be a nice guy."

Shaq up close.

Shaq goes for the stuff.

Shaq takes a breather.

Shaq puts a move on Patrick Ewing.

Jamming time.

Larry leading UNLV to their NCAA title.

Courtesy Charlotte Hornets

Larry's a happy man.

Larry holds his ground against Larry Bird.

Larry on a breakaway.

Who is that Grandmama?

LARRY JOHNSON

1

The Toughest Battle

Larry Johnson's rise to NBA stardom, and the big-time money that goes with it, has been as sure and smooth as a magic carpet ride. The six-year, 20-million-dollar contract that he signed with the Charlotte Hornets allowed Larry to buy a large house on Lake Wylie, in the affluent community of Riverpointe, North Carolina. It also gave him the means to fill his garage with fancy cars, and stock his home with video arcade games, a pool table, and a monster stereo system.

Larry was also able to buy a penthouse high above the city of Dallas, a few minutes and a million miles away from the nasty neighborhood where he grew up. Because long before Larry began bringing in the big bucks for banging bodies with the Charles Barkleys of the world, he had to fight an even tougher battle on the desperate streets of South Dallas.

The poverty-stricken Dixon Circle projects where Larry lived with his mother and sister were a breeding ground for criminal behavior. The area was so infested with drugs and violence that it was named the War Zone, and it was constantly reaching out to swallow up new lives. Business in the Zone was so brisk, the local police precinct set up a station right in the middle of the projects. "Each house had its own specialty," recalls Larry. "There was the crack house, the coke house, the weed house, and one for prostitution. There was a guy out there who got paid just to direct the traffic. One guy would get out of his car, make a deal, and another would be waiting right behind him."

In addition to crime, street fighting was a way of life on those mean streets. "You'd have a fight once a week," says

Larry. "If you played Monday through Saturday and didn't have a fight you knew you had to get ready for Sunday."

The battle to stay straight when violence and drugs were sucking the life force out of the neighborhood was constant. "Guys I grew up with who weren't into drugs then are into them now," says Larry. But while other kids crashed on crack, Larry spent his time shooting baskets at the Redbird Recreational Center and at Green Bay Park, the one-hoop court smack in the middle of the projects.

You could almost always find Larry going full-tilt in the slam-jamming games that went on throughout the day. "I was always playing with older kids. Those older kids were more intimidating to me then than the people I'm playing against now. I was a little kid. Those guys on the playground were taller, stronger, meaner."

Even after the other players would call it a night, Larry and his best friend, Air Greg Williams, would go on playing one-on-one on the dimly lit court. "I always knew where I could find Larry," says his mother Dortha. "I'd just look out the window, even at three o'clock in the morning, and he'd be on the court playing basketball."

Larry's determination to avoid the dead-end world of drugs allowed him to live out his big dreams, and has also set a life-saving example to the other children in the Zone. "Larry serves as a prime role model for what we are trying to teach and coach," said Ed Wesley, who coached Larry at Hood Middle School. Wesley points at two large posters on the wall of his office, one of Larry in his college uniform and one of him in his Charlotte uniform. "The kids see those posters, and they want to know if Larry Johnson really went to school here. Some of them don't believe me until I get out some of the old team photos—then they get excited. Larry means a lot to us. In this environment, you have the opportunity to go one way or the other. Larry chose the right way. We use his example repeatedly."

"I think Larry, more than anyone, has helped the situation," says Alex (Mud) Gillum, the director of the Redbird Recreational Center. "Kids have been able to look up to him, to see his success. I think Larry has helped a lot."

Larry has continued to help by operating a summer basketball program at Lincoln High School in South Dallas that provides scholarships for 200 underprivileged children. And when Larry got a call from the Exline recreational center in South Dallas asking if he had any fund-raising ideas to help send the state champion Biddy Basketball team to New Orleans to compete in the national championships, he just wrote out a check and put it in the mail. "He knows that the basketball program keeps the kids off the streets, away from dope and gang activities," said Ronnie Holmes, the volunteer coach of the team. "He knows the situation in the neighborhood. He knew that the kids needed a little help."

"I don't forget home," says Larry.

2

The Biggest Step

Larry was supposed to attend Lincoln High, a black school in South Dallas. But Larry's mom decided that he would be better attending Skyline High, a school on the other side of the city. "My mother made the decision," recalls Larry. "She knew about the discipline at Skyline. She liked that." As Larry tells it, the change in school was the biggest step he ever took. "The toughest adjustment I ever had to make was my first two years at Skyline," says Larry, speaking about going from pick-up games in the street to the disciplined play of organized basketball. "But in every change I've made since, from high school to junior college, from JC to UNLV, and from college to the NBA, what I learned in high school has paid off."

At first, however, it seemed to Larry as though Skyline was on some kind of alien planet. "It was a place totally different from what I knew. All those kids with all those clothes. They called it the Skyline Fashion Show. I'd just look around and watch."

But like the character in the Dr. Seuss story, *What Was I Scared Of?*, Larry seemed as strange to the other 3,500 students as they did to him. "I was the big, scary-looking dude from South Dallas," said Larry, who as a ninth grader was 6–3 and weighed 200 pounds. "I didn't know anyone. I didn't have any real friends. Then basketball season started."

And when it came to hoops, Larry wasn't lacking for confidence. He walked right up to coach J.D. Mayo, introduced himself, and politely expressed the opinion that he was good enough to skip over the freshman and junior varsity teams and just start playing for the varsity.

"Right away you knew he had been raised right," says Mayo. "He had personal values and direction." But having good manners doesn't insure instant stardom on a basketball court. Even Michael Jordan had to wait three years before he earned a varsity letter at his high school. So Coach Mayo just smiled and told Larry to report to the freshman practice. But then a funny thing happened.

On the first day of the season, the three Skyline teams played a triple header against another school. Larry played for the freshman squad, and then sat and watched the junior varsity game. Right before the main event, however, Coach Mayo had a brainstorm. "Why don't I start the kid?" he thought. "Just to see what happens."

What happened was that Larry, playing with and against boys who were two and three years older than he was, went 8-for-8 plus a foul shot in the first half. As the team was walking to the locker room, Larry sidled up to Coach Mayo and asked, "How am I doing, coach?" Mayo chuckled and said, "Larry, if you maintain your great attitude and keep working hard, you're going to be fine."

Larry, who went on to become a four-year starter for Skyline, was a lot better than fine, and no one ever had to worry about Larry's attitude or his work habits. If he wasn't at the Redbird Recreation Center he was at the hoop in Green Bay Park. Even on Friday nights when most everyone was out to parties, Larry and Greg Williams had their own routine. "We'd drive out to Pizza Pizza, pick up two pies and two pints of ice cream," remembers Greg. "We'd park the car at the same place every week, sit on the fender in our gym clothes, and eat. We'd talk with everyone, see who could make the other one laugh the most. Then we'd go across the street to the court."

Larry's hard work and dedication paid off in a big way in his senior season. In addition to being named a high school

3

Player of the Year

Although Larry had been recruited by colleges all across the country, he decided to stay in Dallas and accept a scholarship from SMU. But after a question arose about his SAT scores, Larry decided to short-circuit the controversy and enroll at Odessa Junior College.

When Larry arrived at Odessa, the West Texas town was well past the boom days when the oil wells that dot Odessa had pumped black gold out of the ground. The wells had already gone bone dry, shrinking both the local economy and the spirit of the people. Larry's play, though, gave the towns-folk something to cheer about for a change, while putting Odessa on the collegiate basketball map.

In his first season at Odessa, Larry averaged 22 points, 18.1 rebounds, and 3.1 blocked shots per game, while leading OJC to a 32–5 record, and a junior college regional championship. "I had heard a lot about Larry Johnson," said Odessa assistant coach, Lonnie Thompson. "But I didn't believe it until I saw his first game." Larry quickly turned everyone into an instant believer, as he went on to earn the Junior College Player of the Year award, and he was also named the top freshman player in the country by the *Sporting News* and *Basketball Times*. "When he gets the ball, sometimes I just stop and watch to see what he'll do next," said point guard Tony Jackson, Larry's teammate at OJC. One amazing move that Larry wowed his teammates with at practice was a spectacular dunk. He would bounce the ball off the wall behind the backboard; jump up; catch it; and then **jam** it.

Larry, as usual, shunned the party routine, and instead concentrated on getting himself ready for the bigger challenges that lay ahead. "I just played ball, worked hard, and went back to my dorm room."

About the only misgiving Larry felt about going to a small, out-of-the-limelight school was when he sat in the lobby at OJC and watched the big-time teams beamed in on a cable television station. "I would watch Sam Higgins and Dennis Scott, guys I had played with at the McDonalds All-American Game. I would watch and think, 'Oh man, I should be up there.' But I wasn't about to let myself get buried. I love the game too much."

Larry continued to move toward his dream of playing in the NBA during his sophomore season at OJC, as he averaged 28.3 points and 17.3 rebounds per game, while leading Odessa to a 33–2 record, a second successive regional championship, and the No. 2 ranking among junior college teams. Larry, who played like a man among boys, pocketed his second straight Junior College Player of the Year trophy, and was also named the 1989 USA Basketball Athlete of the Year, becoming the first junior college player to receive that award.

Although OJC hadn't been Larry's first choice, he had stayed with the program and, with his upbeat attitude, made the situation work to his benefit. "In high school, you don't want to go to a junior college because of the lack of publicity. My thing was, I didn't think there was any talent here, that it was a step down. It really wasn't, though. You know, this turned out to be the best thing that could have happened to me."

4

Number One

Once again, the big-time college scouts came calling, including Jerry Tarkanian, who was coaching at the University of Nevada Las Vegas. What grabbed Tarkanian's attention, over and above the obviously extraordinary talent, was Larry's work ethic and the positive attitude that he projected. The coach was also impressed with how Larry had acted in a summer league tournament in Dallas. Although Larry could have put together an all-star team of top-flight college players whose skills would have helped to showcase his own talents, Larry instead picked a team from among his old high school friends and acquaintances. And despite the handicap, Larry still managed to lead his team to a first-place finish.

Tarkanian was so hot for Larry to come to UNLV that, according to Mark Warkenstein, the school's former recruiting coordinator, "Jerry spent more time recruiting Larry than he did on all of the other players combined during my seven years at UNLV."

Steve Green, the coach at Howard Junior College, knew just why Tarkanian was spending so much time wooing Larry. "I've yet to see anything he can't do. He handles the ball, shoots it, and rebounds like a mad man. He just makes all the big plays. In my opinion, he'll take the Rebels from wherever they are and turn them into a top five team."

While Larry was impressed with Tarkanian, the major selling point for him was that he had grown friendly with two UNLV players at the tryouts for the 1988 Olympic Team. "I love the guys on that team," said Larry, referring to point guard Greg Anthony and defensive ace Stacey Augmon, whom Larry had first met and formed a friendship with two years earlier when they had played for the US team at the World Junior Championships in Italy.

Although he was about to go from a small-town, junior-college atmosphere, to the bright lights of Las Vegas and the intense pressure of big-time college basketball, Larry wasn't at all anxious. "If you're prepared for the situation, you don't have to be nervous. It's only when you're not prepared that you have to worry. I'll do a lot of running. I'll work on defense and with the weights. I know for sure, I'll come prepared. After that, whatever happens, happens."

Tark the Shark, meanwhile, was licking his lips at the thought of Larry leading UNLV to the top of the college rankings. "I think coming into school, he'll be the best player we ever recruited. We've never had a kid with these kinds of accomplishments. Right now, he's better than anybody we have. With Larry in the lineup, we can compete against any team in the country."

With Larry added to a team that already included Augmon, Anthony, the sharp-shooting Anderson Hunt, and center David Butler, the Rebels didn't just compete, they crushed most of their competition while posting a 26–5 record during the 1989–1990 season. The Rebels then romped to the Big West conference title, beating their three opponents by an average margin of more than 22 points per game, while Larry pulled down the tourney's MVP trophy after he had already collected the Conference Player of the Year award. And then it was time for a little March Madness, as the Rebels capped their season with six straight NCAA tournament wins, including a 103–73 demolition of Duke that brought UNLV their first NCAA championship. It was the first time that a team had ever gone over the century mark in the finals, and the 30-point margin of victory also set an NCAA championship game record.

Larry, meanwhile, had lived up to all of the advance notices which had heralded him as the best recruit in UNLV history. Using his full repertoire of talents, Larry not only set a school single-season rebounding record while also leading the team in scoring, field goal percentage, and free throw accuracy, but he also became the first consensus All-American in UNLV history. "Larry is the most complete player I have ever coached," said Tarkanian. "He literally can do everything—score, rebound, pass, and defend—and he does them all exceptionally well. He can dominate a game from start to finish."

In addition to his phenomenal physical skills, Larry also brought a verve and enthusiasm onto the court that got picked up by his teammates and also helped to fuel the Runnin' Rebels' ride to the top of the college basketball world. "I just wish he'd stop smiling," joked the late Jim Valvano, the former coach of the North Carolina State Wolfpack. "It's bad enough he's tearing us up without enjoying it so much."

While Larry was tough on his opponents, he was, unlike a lot of stars, unusually considerate toward his teammates. On Senior Day at UNLV, for example, Larry sat himself down early in a game against Louisville to make sure that his backup, senior Moses Scurry, would get extra playing time.

"We had five starters returning from a team that went to the quarterfinals of the NCAA tournament one year before, and Larry comes in and he's beat the best of the bunch," said Tarkanian. "That could have been an explosive situation. But Larry came in and handled it so well. He's a team man in every way."

Larry also showed that he had more on his mind than basketball; when UNLV was invited to the White House, Larry took the opportunity to tell then-President Bush that he wasn't doing enough to help the poor people in the country.

5

Time To Decide

A lot of people thought that Larry would leave UNLV and ride the wave of his great season right into the NBA, fulfilling his boyhood dream of becoming a professional basketball player. The decision to enter the NBA draft was seemingly made easier because of the threat of NCAA sanctions hanging over UNLV's head for alleged violations in past recruiting practices. If the sanctions were invoked, it would mean that the Rebels wouldn't be allowed to defend their NCAA title. Larry also had to take into account all the money he would be passing up if he stayed in school for a fourth year, and whether the pot of gold would be anywhere near as big the following year. "I think there's a time when a guy is just right to come out of college and enter the NBA draft," advised Don Nelson, the coach and general manager of the Golden State Warriors. "Everything is just right for Johnson now. The money is there; the maturity is there; his team won the NCAA championship; it's just time."

Larry, though, must have had a different clock. Because after talking over the situation with coach Tarkanian, and with his mother, who advised him to stay in school while leaving the final decision up to him, Larry decided to return to UNLV for his senior season, as did Stacey Augmon, who faced a similar situation. "Going to school and playing basketball is a great thing to do," declared Larry.

"Larry is a truly remarkable individual," said Tarkanian. "He could have taken the NBA money and run, but he decided to return get his degree. Larry Johnson is what college athletics is all about."

In July, when the word came down that UNLV would definitely be banned from postseason play, Larry and Stacey again had the chance to turn pro, either by petitioning the NBA for a special draft, or by accepting the multi-million dollars being waved in front of them by European basketball teams. Larry and Stacey, and the other seniors on the UNLV team, also had the option of transferring to another college and going after another NCAA crown.

But Larry and the others felt too much loyalty toward Tarkanian to desert what looked like a sinking ship. "If we can't play for a title, then we'll play for pride," said Stacey. "We're all about playing our hearts out and winning games, not trophies," added Larry.

Larry also took the time to call his coach and make sure that all was well with Tark. "On the phone, all Larry wanted to know was how *I* was doing. Was *I* all right."

Although no one could have guessed it at the time, the NCAA reversed itself in November, postponing the post-season ban that would have prevented the Runnin' Rebels from competing in the 1991 NCAA tournament.

6

Getting Ready

During Larry's last season at UNLV, he spent a lot of time working on his outside shot. He was already the premier power forward in the collegiate ranks, but, at only 6–5½, Larry knew that he would have to improve his perimeter shooting and driving ability to become an NBA superstar.

So Larry put in a lot of one-on-one practice time against his best friend, Stacey Augmon, who had won the Henry Iba Corinthian Award as the best defender in college basketball. The man-to-man workouts bettered both their games and deepened their mutual respect and friendship. "I can't get around him," complained Larry. "If I do it once I'm happy. He eats you up alive." Stacey, though, shot the praise right back at his practice partner. "Aw, Larry's too tough. He's always getting his shot off. Larry's the only guy strong enough to stick me."

Larry's respect and affection for Stacey is so special that he dedicated his senior season to trying to help his friend gain the recognition that Larry felt had been lacking. "I'm going to help make Stacey Augmon the Player of the Year. We all help each other on this team, and that's what makes being at UNLV so great. There are no big egos with us."

That all-for-one attitude helped propel the Runnin' Rebels to a 30–0 record on their way to the No. 1 ranking in college ball, and a return trip to the Final Four. They were such an overpowering quintet that virtually everyone considered them to be a shoo-in to become the first team to repeat as NCAA champions since UCLA won the last of its seven straight titles in 1973. In fact, Kentucky coach Rick Pitino wasn't alone in suggesting that the Rebels—who had trailed for a total of 81 seconds out of 680 second-half minutes during the season—would have to enter the NBA to find teams to compete against.

But in one of the major upsets in NCAA tournament history, Duke, the eventual champion, turned the tables on UNLV, defeating them 79–77. The semifinals loss to a team that they destroyed in the finals only a year earlier brought UNLV's super season to a sorry finish. Despite the disappointing ending to a season that had been filled with victories, Larry swept all of the major trophies, including the John R. Wooden, James A. Naismith and *Sporting News* Player of the Year awards. "He has a completeness about his play in every phase of the game that is so unique, it allows him to do anything he wants to do on the court, offensively or defensively," said San Jose State coach Stan Morrison. "I've never seen a player who has so many things he could do to help his team."

And even more than the *ability* to help his team, and even beyond the wins and the awards, the legacy that Larry left behind at UNLV was his *willingness* to be a team player and a caring human being. "His greatest strength is that he helps his team win," said Tarkanian. "He unites whatever team he's on and they're going to win eventually because everyone is going to be happy. They're all going to play together.

"If Larry has a lay-up he's going to give it to the other guy every time. Not once in a while. Every time. Not once in his two-year career did I ever see him look at a stat sheet.

"He's a unique individual."

7

Top Choice

With his college career behind him, Larry began to look forward to playing professionally, hoping that he would be selected by the Dallas Mavericks in the NBA draft so that he would get to play in front of his family and hometown friends. Larry's mom also had her fingers crossed. "If he's in Dallas, playing at the Arena, all I have to do is go right down," said Dortha. "I won't have to drive five or six hours, like I've been doing."

But once the order of selection was settled and the Mavs wound up with the sixth pick in the 1991 draft, everyone knew that there was no way that Larry was going to be playing his home games in Reunion Arena.

Charlotte, the team with the No. 1 pick, seemed to be a likely landing spot for Larry, but there was a split in the Hornets hierarchy—some voices were calling out for Billy Owens, the versatile forward from Syracuse University, while others had set their sights on Dikembe Mutombo, the 7–1 center from Georgetown University, by way of Zaire. Mutombo was also the overwhelming favorite among Hornet fans, according to a newspaper poll conducted by the Charlotte Observer.

But Allen Bristow, the Hornets' director of player personnel who was about to become the team's head coach, was a big Larry Johnson fan. Bristow liked Larry's hard-driving style of play. He also noticed that Larry had been the player of the year at every level he had competed at, and that he had led every team that he ever played on to a title. That individual talent and toughness, fused with his demonstrated ability to turn teams into champions, is what ultimately caused the Hornets to spend their No. 1 pick on Larry.

"Larry Johnson is a quality player, a competitor and a guy with a tough mentality which separated him from the rest of the candidates," explained Bristow. "Most of all, he's a winner."

Although Larry was initially disappointed that he wouldn't be playing in Dallas, he was thrilled at being the No. 1 pick, and he was looking forward to the challenge of playing against the world's best basketball players. "Of course those guys are going to be bigger and stronger than college players, so I'm going to have to work a little harder.

"I'll basically offer the Charlotte Hornets what I've always offered the teams I've played on—hard work, doing whatever I'm asked to do, whatever my teammates need me to do, and just try to win."

Winning, though, wouldn't come easily, even for Larry, with a sad-sack team like Charlotte, which had been the Central Division doormat in each of its three years in the NBA, and had ended the 1990–91 season with a dismal 26–56 record.

Because of the extended negotiating, Larry didn't actually sign a contract with Charlotte until the end of training camp, which prevented him from practicing with his new teammates or properly preparing for the upcoming season. Larry was going to be forced to undergo on-the-job training, learning to play with his own team as well as against the other teams in the league. But Larry had always been a King on the basketball court, and he wasn't about to abdicate. "I knew back then that I was going to make my mark for myself and my team. People said I was the best in junior college, the best in college. I wasn't ready to stop there. I want to be one of those guys people talk about when they say, 'He won at this level.' I want all of that."

Before Larry began fulfilling those personal dreams,

though, he made sure that thousands of other people would have a brighter day by making a $180,000 donation to the United Way of Central Carolinas, the largest contribution ever made by an athlete to the organization. "I don't know if he's got a fan club yet," said Bill Corley, the local campaign person. But I'm ready to start one. This would be a great gift in any year, but it's particularly meaningful because we were in trouble. I've never seen a more difficult time to raise money. Not only did Larry have the resources, but he also had the heart."

But just because Larry had begun to generously share his new-found wealth, it didn't mean that his teammates weren't going to put him through the wringer of rookie initiation rites. Since the veterans hadn't had the chance to spring any pranks on Larry during training camp, they snared him with a good one right before the team's home opener at the sold-out Charlotte Coliseum. Just before the Hornets were supposed to take the floor, guard Del Curry told Larry that it was a tradition for a rookie to lead the team onto the court. So while Larry charged out onto the hardwood and received a standing ovation, the rest of the team stayed in the tunnel, doubled over with laugher as Larry discovered that he was the only player on the court.

Larry's first NBA action had come the night before against the great Larry Bird and the Celtics on the famous parquet floor at the Boston Garden. Although Charlotte dropped the game 111–108, and Larry was limited to 14 points and three rebounds, the Hornets realized that they were playing with a warrior. As guard Kendall Gill noted, "He was a rookie for one day." Larry also took a treasured memento away from the game, a picture of him with Bird that hangs in Larry's home. "I'm really sorry that Magic Johnson retired before I had a chance to get a picture that I could hang up next to the one with Bird and me," said Larry, who has a sense of tradition about the game and a deep respect for its great players.

A few weeks after that first game, the Celtics came to Charlotte and Bird tossed in 25 points and pulled down 11 rebounds. But Larry was just a little bit better, threading the nets for 27 points and ripping off 15 boards while leading the Hornets to a rare victory. "Larry is strong, quick, and very aggressive," declared Bird. "He gets better position than anybody else in the league. He's powerful, and when he gets the ball, he can jump over anybody. He's a great player and I give him all the respect in the world." Which was heady praise from one of the all-time greats of the game to a rookie who hadn't even completed his first month in the league.

8

Rookie of the Year

In the NBA, there are always games within the game, with players battling to attain dominance like a couple of antelopes locking horns. Players are constantly testing each other, trying to gain the physical or psychological edge that will allow them to control a match-up.

Larry found out about this aspect of life in the NBA in the Hornets' home opener when Derrick Coleman, the New Jersey Nets' 6–10 power forward, tried to take the rookie to school. Coleman, who had been the previous No. 1 pick in the draft and was coming off a Rookie of the Year season, tried to send a message early on by calling for the ball in a position that isolated him one-on-one against Larry. Larry, though, didn't give an inch. "Iso? You're not going to take me to the hole," he told Coleman. "I've got to talk," says Larry. "It makes me play harder." Larry played so hard that even though Coleman outscored him, 17–16, Larry won the battle of the boards by a lopsided 18–9 margin, registering the first double-double of his NBA career. "No one intimidates me," declared Larry. "I'm not the best player in the league, but I'm not intimidated. In the Dixon neighborhood where I learned the game, if you didn't play tough, you didn't last long." Then he flashed his infectious smile and added, "But you have to have fun when you play. That's what it's all about."

"He's way ahead of my expectations," said teammate Kendall Gill. "I didn't think he'd start *this* fast. And I certainly didn't expect 18 rebounds. Wow!"

Although Larry is only 6–5½, he is, as coach Bristow points out, "A terrific rebounder. His heart measures bigger than his height." Larry does have unusually long arms and he's also very quick and a great leaper, as well as being exceptionally strong. At 250 pounds of mostly muscle that Larry has been building since his high school days, it's next to impossible to move him once he establishes position. "He's like a tree," notes Philadelphia 76ers forward Armon Gilliam. "It's so hard to root him out."

Lenny Wilkens, the newly-appointed coach of the Atlanta Hawks, compares Larry to the Detroit Pistons' Dennis Rodman, who has led the league in rebounding for the past two seasons. "Johnson is big and strong, while Rodman is skinny. But they both get the job done because they work hard and pursue the ball." Paul Silas, an assistant coach with the Nets, stresses Larry's rebounding technique. "How you use your body is very important," says Silas, who retired as one of the NBA's all-time leading boardmen with 12,357 rebounds. "He's always holding people off with his shoulder or his forearm, and that's how you retain position."

To the Phoenix Suns' forward Charles Barkley, another undersized rebounding leader and the player with whom Larry is most often compared, rebounding comes down to one essential—desire. "Technique is good," says Sir Charles, the NBA's 1993 MVP. "But you still have to get the ball. That's what it's all about, and that's what Larry Johnson does. He's a hell of a player."

Game after game, Larry's rebounding and scoring gave the Hornets consistency on which they could lean. In his first 34 games in the NBA, he had a double-double (putting up double-figure totals in two different statistical categories, such as rebounding and scoring) in 22 of them. "What sets Larry apart is his dependability," said Bristow. "Most rookies go up and down in their performances, they have a great game, then a bad one. Larry's been very consistent, and his game will continue to grow. He's getting powerful numbers now, but he understands he can do even more. You see the difference every game; he gets better and better."

Larry, though, still wasn't interested in individual stats or personal glory divorced from team success. "The double-doubles are great—if they help us win. I feel I have the skill to get double-doubles every game, but my totals don't really matter if the Hornets don't win."

Larry's play and hard work also set an example for his mates, while his attitude set the tone for the team; and as a result, he became—astonishingly—the leader of the Hornets only three months into his rookie season. "A leader is tough to find," said Bristow. "It's an intangible that a lot of teams don't have. Look at the Lakers without Magic, and the Celtics without Bird. We have a leader now, not a loud leader, but a mature one who leads by example. Larry's a guy we know we can build our franchise around. He's our building block, our foundation."

Although Larry had become the leader of the Hornets, they were still a team that lost a lot more than they won, and a great deal more than Larry was used to. In his two *seasons* at UNLV, Larry was on the losing side only *six* times in 75 games. In his first two *weeks* with Charlotte, he was on the short side of the score *seven* times. "I used to say that if you can go out and play 110 percent but lose, you should feel good because you did all you could," says Larry. "But what I say and what I feel are two different things. It's hard for me to lose. Even back in the pick-up games at Dixon, sometimes I would cry after a loss.

"I just keep thinking in the back of my mind about how it's going to feel when we start winning night after night. But for right now, I'll just have to take what's there and run with it."

Which is exactly what Larry did, as he kept running the floor, banging the boards, and putting the ball in the basket.

Larry had a lot of memorable games along the way, including a 31-point torching of the NBA champion Chicago Bulls.

"He sure doesn't play like a rookie," declared Bulls superstar Michael Jordan. "He's aggressive, and plays with a lot of confidence, like he's been in the league a long time. Larry's going to be in the top five percent of NBA players—if he's not already," added his Airness.

"Larry Johnson is a rock," declared Chicago forward Horace Grant, the player who had tried to guard him. "I think he'll be an All-Star very soon."

But the game that Larry sites as his most satisfying of the season was a nail-biter against the Super Sonics in Seattle. During the pre-game practice, Bristow had installed a new play—dubbed "Dallas"—which was designed to isolate Larry on the defender late in a game in a do-or-die situation. That night, Bristow called for the "Dallas" play with only seven tenths of a second left on the clock, and Larry responded by draining a buzzer-beating turnaround jumper that gave the Hornets a 117–116 overtime win. "That was a big turning point for me," said Larry. "That was the game that everyone really started showing confidence in me. We started using 'Dallas' a lot after that, which did a lot for my confidence level. I always want to be in the situation where it all depends on what I do on the final shot; I love that."

Larry put on another headline performance during his Dallas homecoming in March, when he lit up the Mavericks for 24 points and 18 rebounds while leading the Hornets to a 120–105 win. It was the first time that Larry had ever played in Reunion Arena, and only the fifth time that he had ever been inside the building. "I didn't have the money then," said Larry, who had given his mom over 100 tickets to distribute to the people of South Dallas. "I had to catch them on TV."

One of the people in the stands rooting for Larry was his high school coach, J.D. Mayo. "We put up a banner at Skyline that has his numeral on it," revealed Mayo. "And there's a stripe for every time he's been named the player of the year at one level or another. I left space at the bottom for an

'NBA Rookie of the Year' stripe. But if he wins the MVP award, I'll have to speak to the principal about putting up another banner."

Although Mayo hasn't had to talk to the principal *yet,* the original banner is striped to the max, because Larry did go on to earn the 1992 NBA Rookie of the Year award in a landslide win over Dikembe Mutombo of the Denver Nuggets. "I remember when I first signed and got off to a slow start, I told Dikembe that even though he had a head start, I was going to come and steal his candy," laughed Larry.

While Larry relished his success, he also knew that he had a stretch of road to travel before he and the Hornets could get where he wanted to go. "Watching the playoffs has been tough. Being a competitor, you just can't help but want to get back out there. But we'll come back next season, work harder, strive for bigger and better things, and hopefully we'll be there next year.

"This season has been a real learning experience," said Larry, who had always been such a dominant player that he could usually count on taking over a game down the stretch. "In the last 10 minutes of a game I'd have everybody leaving the gym thinking about me. In the NBA, it's like—I don't think so.

"I still need to work on my offense, and I need to work on my ball handling and passing skills. I'd like to be one of the best, up there with Magic and Michael, and I'll do whatever it takes to get there."

9

All-Star

"I feel I was born to play basketball," said Larry, after he opened the 1992–93 season with a 29-point explosion that carried the Hornets to an opening-game victory over the Washington Bullets. "I love this game."

By this time, Larry had also decided that he wanted to spend the rest of his career in Charlotte. He liked the sense of being linked to one city the way Bird is with Boston or Magic is with Los Angeles. "I want to play 11, 12 years right here and then retire—but first I want to win some NBA championships, and be the Michael Jordan of Charlotte. This is the team that drafted me, that pays me. This is the place I should be loyal to."

Besides, Larry had grown used to the extra bonuses that can make life around Charlotte so pleasant, especially if you happen to be Larry Johnson. "You get to know all the pizza places," explains Larry. "Sometimes they let me eat free. Sometimes when I call up at midnight and they say they're closing, I tell them who's calling and they decide to stay open late that night. I've got my rental movie places, too. I've got a regular pattern."

Larry could have had the keys to all the pizza stores in Charlotte after it was announced that he had become the first player in the team's history to be voted a starting spot in the NBA All-Star Game. "I thought about being an All-Star five years ago, ten years ago," said Larry. "Ever since I started playing basketball. I tried to imagine myself in the All-Star Game. This is something I want. This is something I dreamed of."

Larry then put his own special touch on the occasion by

buying expensive jackets for every one of his teammates, the coaching staff, and the trainers. "Without their help, I wouldn't be heading for Salt Lake City," the site of the 1993 Game.

It was one thing to dream about being an All-Star, but it didn't compare to the feeling that Larry had on the day before the game when All-Star coach Pat Riley called the starters on the floor for a practice. There he was with Shaquille O'Neal, Scottie Pippin, Isiah Thomas, and Michael Jordan. "He's Air Michael Jordan when he's on my team. When I'm playing against him, though, he's just Michael," quipped Larry.

Although Larry had been voted into the starting line-up by the fans, it was obvious that the league's elite players had also welcomed him into their ranks. "He's a super player," said Karl Malone, the All-Pro power forward of the Utah Jazz. "Larry's so tough, and his quickness is exceptional," added David Robinson, the 7–1 center of the San Antonio Spurs. "A couple of times, he's just posted up and beaten me. You can't be out of position or it's all over. He gets great position, and he has such upper-body strength that he can get the shot off. Then, when you finally get ready for that, he shoots three pointers." As usual, though, Sir Charles found a way to sum up the situation. "He's the future at my position." And then Barkley corrected himself. "The future and the present."

Cleveland center Brad Daugherty, a five-time All-Star, caught another glimpse of Larry, one that had nothing to do with his abilities, but had everything to do with character. "Some All-Star rookies come in here acting like they saved the world. Larry's not like that. He's genuine."

Although Larry already felt like he belonged in the company of the game's greatest players, their praise was warmly welcomed. "A guy wants to be accepted by his peers," explained Larry. "If Michael accepts me, that's more important than scoring 40 points."

While the acclaim was sweet music to Larry's ears, he still had to play third fiddle when it came to his mother, who had come up to see the game. "She's in love with Michael and Shaquille. With them it's, 'Ohhh, Michael. Ohhh Shaquille.' With me it's, 'boy, get your feet off the table.' "

In the game itself, the East lost a hard-played, wild-west overtime shoot-out, 135–132. Larry was also disappointed and angry that he didn't get to contribute as much as he would have liked (four points and four rebounds in 16 minutes), because Pat Riley chose to give the lion's share of the playing time to more experienced, if not more talented, players. But Larry, who knows that was only the first in what will be a long string of All-Star game appearances, quickly turned his attention back to the regular season. "The next thing is, what now? So now what are you going to do?" he asked, pumping himself up.

What Larry did was to go out and join Charles Barkley as the only other player in the NBA to average at least 20 points, 10 rebounds, and four assists. While some players only dream of obtaining an occasional double-double, Larry and Sir Charles had *averaged* it, while playing so unselfishly that they also piled up a substantial number of assists.

Larry also led the league in minutes played, an accomplishment that he attributed to his days on the court at Green Bay Park. "When I was a kid, I played all summer on the asphalt of South Dallas. My feet would get so hot I thought they were going to catch fire. I would be out there seven, eight hours a day, the sweat pouring, but we just kept on playing. I think that's the reason I have so much endurance."

Larry's list of honors continued with his being named to the All-NBA second team, along with established veterans Dominique Wilkins, at the other forward spot, center Patrick Ewing, and guards John Stockton and Joe Dumars. Larry, who was the only second-year player to make the First, Second or Third Teams, beat out both Derrick Coleman and Chicago Bulls star Scottie Pippen, and now ranks behind only Charles Barkley and Karl Malone among all NBA forwards.

More importantly to the team player that Larry is, though, was the fact that he and the Hornets' rookie sensation, center Alonzo Mourning, had led the Hornets to the best record, 44–38, in the team's history and their first appearance in the NBA playoffs.

The Hornets, who ended the season with five straight wins, enabling them to grab the fifth best record in the Eastern Conference, went on to upset the fourth seeded Celtics in the opening round of the playoffs, three games to one. Larry got the Hornets going in the right direction after an opening-game loss in Boston Garden by knocking down the winning shot in a double overtime triumph in the second game that sparked the Hornets to three straight wins in the best-of-five series.

Although the Hornets, the youngest team in the playoffs, couldn't get past a veteran Knicks squad in the second round, they pushed the New Yorkers, the best defensive team in the league, to their limit. While the Knicks took the best-of-seven series, 4–1, none of their wins were by more than four points, except for the first game, which Larry was forced out of with a sprained knee 86 seconds into the first quarter after scoring the Hornets' first two buckets. Although Larry reentered the game late in the third quarter, he was tentative and ineffective. "I definitely think that was the difference," said Alonzo Mourning. "That was a big loss for us. Larry's our best offensive player."

Ultimately, the inexperienced Hornets couldn't quite get it done against a playoff-hardened Knicks team. "It's a new experience for me, playing the same team night in and night out," acknowledged Larry. "I kid the guys on the team that I've got 1,001 moves. I think by now Charles Oakley, Anthony Mason, and Patrick Ewing know all of them. They tell me what I'm going to do before I do it."

But the loss did nothing to diminish Larry's spectacular season, or to darken the future of one of the NBA's brightest young teams. As Kendall Gill pointed out, "It's been a great year. We surprised everyone."

10

A Little Help For His Friends

Superstars have a special quality that draws fans to them as if they generated a magnetic field. With Larry, it's a combination of his powerful game, his genuine niceness, and a smile that can light up a room. "Larry's smile is just contagious," notes George Shinn, the owner of the Charlotte Hornets. "You can't help but like him."

"Larry's simply got a lot of charisma," says Allen Bristow. "He's easy for the fans to like because he's always smiling and having fun, and you sense that deep down there is a good person. And the way he plays has a lot to do with it, too. He always plays with enthusiasm. Fans want to relate to a guy like that."

Larry's popularity has also been helped along by the wonderful commercials that he has done for Converse, in which he plays a slam-jamming Grandmama. The ironic part to the overwhelming success of the commercials is that Larry almost refused to do them, not being real crazy about the idea of dressing up as a woman. "I had my doubts at first. But after a while, I just took it and ran away with it. The ad, since it came out so well, really caught people's eye. There are as many people who know me as 'Grandmama' as Larry Johnson now." And a whole lot more people are about to get introduced to the character, because Grandmama has gone international. The commercials have already run in Australia and Germany, as well as on in-flight videos on American Airlines. And this summer Larry has packed up his dress to promote Converse in France, Spain and Italy. And now there are plans for a video game starring Grandmama, too.

If Larry hadn't agreed to put on a dress, Converse had

another great idea in waiting, according to Larry's agent, Steve Endicott. Larry Bird and Magic Johnson, who also endorse Converse, were going to be scientists in a laboratory, stirring up ingredients to create the next great basketball player. A figure would have appeared out of the smoke and they would have given him a name by combining their own two names: Larry (Bird) (Magic) Johnson. Cute.

Although Larry loves the Grandmama commercials, he would also like to do some others where he could play himself and express his views to children. Children are very important to Larry. He remembers just how hard it can be trying to grow up straight, especially in disadvantaged neighborhoods. That's why Larry takes the time to stop after games and talk to kids and sign autographs. It's also why he operates two basketball camps during the summer, one in South Dallas and the other in Charlotte, and Larry works it out so that most of the children don't have to pay to attend.

Larry tends to be a private person and, especially during the season, a homebody. He doesn't smoke, do drugs, or drink, and he would rather spend his time at home, getting the proper rest, than staying out late in bars or nightclubs. Outside of his teammates, Larry has only three close friends: Greg Williams, whom he has known since fourth grade; Stacey Augmon, his UNLV teammate, who now stars for the Atlanta Hawks; and Ken Roberson, a personal trainer and guru. "I can be sitting on his couch with him and leave there feeling that I've learned things," says Larry. Roberson, who advises Larry about health, nutrition, and life in general, emphasizes responsible behavior, especially towards women. "I feel to disrespect any woman is to curse one's own existence, because we all come from a woman."

Although Larry enjoys his privacy, he also likes to go out and meet people. "I love the popularity," says Larry. "I really love it." And Larry is so popular that his number 2 Charlotte

Hornets jersey is second in worldwide sales, trailing only the number 23 of Michael Jordan's Chicago Bulls shirt.

Larry's popularity, clean living, and great playing has also made him the ideal spokesperson for NBA Authentics, a line of clothing promoted by the league. "We feel that Larry has a tremendous future in the NBA, and we want to focus a great deal of attention on him," said Rick Welts, the president of NBA Properties. Larry, for his part, enjoys the responsibility of representing the NBA. "It's an honor and a privilege," said Larry, who is only the third player after Magic Johnson and Isiah Thomas to serve as the spokesperson for the line. "That's a goal of mine—to be one of the guys who takes the league to another level and be one of the premiere players, the perennial superstars.

"I don't mind the publicity, or the fact that if I do anything wrong it hits the paper. I don't mind, because I don't plan on doing anything wrong."

And when Larry thinks it's past his time in the NBA, he imagines going back to the Dixon Circle in South Dallas. The projects have been torn down, but the basketball court is still there, and Larry contemplates building a recreation center around it. "I want to do something helpful. Ain't no telling how many little Larry's can come out of Dixon."

Sources

Sports Illustrated
The Charlotte Observer
The New York Times
The Orlando Sentinel
The Sporting News

SHAQUILLE O'NEAL

Birthdate: March 6, 1972
Birthplace: Newark, New Jersey

Height: 7-1
Weight: 303

LSU STATS

YEAR	G/GS	FG/FGA	PCT	FT/FTA	PCT	REB	AVG	PF/D	AST	TO	BLK	STL	PTS	AVG
1989–90	32/28	180/314	.573	85/153	.556	385	12.0	122/9	61	93	115	38	445	13.9
1990–91	28/28	312/497	.628	150/235	.638	411	14.7	79/1	45	99	140	41	774	27.6
1991–92	30/30	294/478	.615	134/254	.528	421	14.0	86/5	46	103	157	29	722	24.1
TOTALS	90/86	786/1289	.610	369/642	.575	1217	13.5	287/15	152	295	412	108	1941	21.6

NBA REGULAR SEASON STATS

YEAR–TEAM	G	MIN	FGM	FGA	PCT	FTM	FTA	PCT	OFF	DEF	TOT	AST	PF	DQ	STL	BLK	PTS	AVG
1992–93 Orl	81	3071	733	1304	.562	427	721	.592	342	780	1122	152	321	8	60	286	1893	23.4

LARRY JOHNSON

Birthdate: March 14, 1969

Birthplace: Tyler, Texas

Height: 6–5½

Weight: 250

UNLV STATS

YEAR	G/GS	FG/FGA	PCT	3PT FG/FGA	PCT	FT/FTA	PCT	REBOUNDS OFF	DEF	TOT	AVG	AST	TO	BLK	STL	PTS	AVG
1989–90	40/40	304/487	.624	13/38	.342	201/262	.767	151	306	457	11.4	84	110	56	65	822	20.6
1990–91	35/35	308/465	.662	17/48	.354	162/198	.818	147	233	380	10.9	104	78	36	74	795	22.7
TOTALS	75/75	612/952	.643	30/86	.349	363/460	.789	298	539	837	11.2	188	188	92	139	1617	21.6

NBA REGULAR SEASON STATS

YEAR–TEAM	G	MIN	FGM	FGA	PCT	FTM	FTA	PCT	REB	REBOUNDS OFF	DEF	TOT	AVG	AST	PF	STL	TO	BLK	PTS	AVG
91–92 Cha	82	3047	616	1258	.490	339	409	.829	899					292	225	81	160	51	1576	19.2
92–93 Cha	82	3323	728	1385	.526	336	438	.767	864					353	187	53	227	27	1810	22.1
TOTALS	164	6370	1344	2643	.509	675	847	.797	1763					645	412	134	387	78	3386	20.6

3-point FG: 1991–92, 5–22 (.277); 1992–93, 18–71 (.254) TOTALS: 23–93 (.247)

NBA PLAYOFF STATS

YEAR–TEAM	G	GS	MIN	FG	FGA	PCT	3-POINT FG	FG	FGA	PCT	FT	FTA	PCT	REBOUNDS OFF	DEF	TOT	AST	PF	DQ	STL	TO	BLK	PTS	AVG
1993 Cha	9	9	348	68	122	.557		1	4	.250	41	52	.788	19	43	62	30	27	0	5	19	2	178	19.8

You might want to order some of our other exciting sports titles:

BASEBALL SUPERSTARS ALBUM 1993, by Richard J. Brenner. Includes Frank Thomas, Juan Gonzales, Paul Molitor, Roberto Alomar, Barry Larkin, Ryne Sandberg, Fred McGriff and ten more baseball superstars. 48 pages including 16 in full color. ($4.00/5.00 Canada)

FOOTBALL SUPERSTARS ALBUM 1993, by Richard J. Brenner. Includes Troy Aikman, Emmitt Smith, Barry Sanders, Steve Young, Warren Moon, Jerry Rice, Junior Seau and ten more football superstars. 48 pages including 16 in full color. ($4.00/5.00 Canada)

BASKETBALL SUPERSTARS ALBUM 1993, by Richard J. Brenner. Includes Michael Jordan, Magic Johnson, David Robinson, Charles Barkley, John Stockton, Larry Johnson, Horace Grant and ten more basketball superstars. 48 pages including 16 in full color. ($4.00/5.00 Canada)

THE WORLD SERIES, The Great Contests, by Richard J. Brenner. The unique excitement of the World Series is brought to life in seven of the most thrilling contests ever played, including the 1991 and 1992 Series. 160 pages, including 16 action-packed photos. ($3.50/4.50 Canada)

THE COMPLETE SUPER BOWL STORY, Games I-XXVII, by Richard J. Brenner. The most exciting moments in Super Bowl history are brought to life, game by game. 208 pages, including 16 memorable photos. ($3.50/4.50 Canada)

SHAQUILLE O'NEAL*LARRY JOHNSON, by Richard J. Brenner. A dual biography of the two brightest young stars in basketball. 96 pages, 10 pages of photos. ($3.50/4.50 Canada)

BARRY BONDS*ROBERTO ALOMAR, by Bob Woods. A dual biography of two of baseball's best players. 96 pages, 10 pages of photos ($3.50/4.50 Canada)

ISIAH THOMAS*CHARLES BARKLEY, by Jordan Deutsch. A lively look at two NBA superstars. 96 pages, 12 photos. ($2.95/3.75 Canada)

MARIO LEMIEUX, by Richard J. Brenner. An exciting biography of hockey's greatest player. 96 pages, 10 pages of photos ($3.50/4.50 Canada)

BRETT HULL, by M.J. Goldstein. An easy-to-read biography of the top goal scorer in the NHL over the last three seasons. 48 pages. Lots of exciting photos. Complete career stats. ($3.00/4.00 Canada)

MICHAEL JORDAN, by Richard J. Brenner. An easy-to-read, photo-filled biography especially for young readers. 32 pages. ($3.00/4.00 Canada)

WAYNE GRETZKY, by Richard J. Brenner. An easy-to-read, photo-filled biography of hockey's top star. 32 pages. ($3.00/4.00 Canada)

ORDER FORM

Please indicate the number of copies of each title that you are ordering.

_____	BASEBALL SUPERSTARS ALBUM 1993	($4.00/5.00 Canada)
_____	FOOTBALL SUPERSTARS ALBUM 1993	($4.00/5.00 Canada)
_____	BASKETBALL SUPERSTARS ALBUM 1993	($4.00/5.00 Canada)
_____	THE WORLD SERIES	($3.50/4.50 Canada)
_____	THE COMPLETE SUPER BOWL STORY	($3.50/4.50 Canada)
_____	SHAQUILLE O'NEAL*LARRY JOHNSON	($3.50/4.50 Canada)
_____	BARRY BONDS*ROBERTO ALOMAR	($3.50/4.50 Canada)
_____	ISIAH THOMAS*CHARLES BARKLEY	($2.95/3.95 Canada)
_____	MARIO LEMIEUX	($3.50/4.50 Canada)
_____	BRETT HULL	($3.00/4.00 Canada)
_____	MICHAEL JORDAN	($3.00/4.00 Canada)
_____	WAYNE GRETZKY	($3.00/4.00 Canada)

Payment must accompany all orders. *All payments must be in U.S. dollars.*
Postage and handling is $1.35 per book up to a maximum of $6.75. ($1.75 to a maximum of $8.75 in Canada.)

TOTAL NUMBER OF BOOKS ORDERED _____
TOTAL COST OF BOOKS $_____
POSTAGE AND HANDLING $_____
TOTAL COST OF ORDER $_____

Please don't forget to enclose a check or money order in U.S. funds only.
Please make checks payable to: EAST END PUBLISHING, Ltd.
54 Alexander Dr.
Syosset, NY 11791

Discounts are available on orders of 25 or more copies. For details, call: (516-364-6383).

Please print neatly.

NAME: _____

ADDRESS: _____

CITY: _____ STATE: _____ ZIP CODE: _____

PLEASE ALLOW FOUR WEEKS FOR DELIVERY.

Send to: East End Publishing, Ltd., Dept. SB3, 54 Alexander Drive, Syosset, NY 11791 USA.